Here's a
Hero—
Joseph

Jim —
Hero!
Do it !

Lee Morgan

Here's a
Hero—
Joseph

Les Morgan

CHRISTIAN PUBLICATIONS
CAMP HILL, PENNSYLVANIA

*To my good friend, Fred Hartley,
who took time to be a hero
when I so desperately needed one
and whose lifestyle defines a "hero"*

Christian Publications
3825 Hartzdale Drive, Camp Hill, PA 17011

The mark of  *vibrant faith*

ISBN: 0-87509-428-7
LOC Catalog Card Number: 89-82276
© 1990 by Christian Publications
All rights reserved
Printed in the United States of America

90 91 92 93 94   5 4 3 2 1

Cover: sculptural illustration by Deb Troyer Bunnell
Cartoon illustrations by Simeon Dawster

C O N T E N T S

PREFACE

In a day when wrong is being called right, when *stability* is a word your grandmother used, when people are seen as objects and when dignity and respect have been traded for a way to turn a fast buck, it is refreshing to find a hero who proves to be genuine, even when no one is looking. Joseph is that hero.

Though rejected and ripped off, lied about and forgotten, tempted and forsaken, he shines as a light in a dark world, showing us how to live triumphantly even when we've been used and then discarded. In Joseph we find a man who displays integrity and honesty even though no one is handing out awards. His walk with the Lord is insightful, proving that when God is looking for models of greatness, He often chooses teenagers. Through it all, Joseph is consistent, making him the hero we all so desperately need.

I trust that the work invested in this book will prove to be helpful to you. I deeply appreciate my good friend, Fred Hartley, for his encouragement, not only in this project but also in being a hero to me in my teen years. To him I warmly dedicate this book. The foreword by Jay Strack is an honor that I could have only dreamed about. To him I express gratitude. I am thankful to Kay, my wife, who faithfully stood by me as I carved out this material, encouraging me all the way. I am also indebted to Candace McKelvey and Crystal Reece, my secretaries who assisted in many ways throughout the writing and editorial process. I am also grateful to the people at Christian Publications for their commitment to me as a writer and coworker. Finally I am thankful to the Lord for what He has done in my own life as well as in the lives of those who first heard this as a series at Campus Community Church, a great fellowship of which I am privileged to be the pastor.

May the Lord use this book to restore hope and life to those who feel the sting of rejection, and raise up heroes to amaze the world. He did it once in the life of a teen named Joseph. May He do it again for His glory.

Les Morgan
Toccoa Falls College
Toccoa, Georgia

FOREWORD

■■■■■■■

In a day when heroes are on the endangered species list, Les Morgan not only teaches us of the lives and inspiration of many heroes, but in doing so he teaches us how to become a hero.

I have stated for years that the greatest truth that you can teach a teenager is the ability to stand alone – to resist the tug of the crowd. Les Morgan has accomplished this. He effectively alternates illustrations from the life of Joseph with contemporary lives that are as up-to-date as tomorrow's newspapers.

Parents as well as teens will find the questions at the end of each chapter a great help in transferring truths.

Methods and gimmicks grow stale and dusty, but eternal principles live forever. This book on Joseph is full of principles that will protect and prosper.

This is without question the finest book I have read on the life of Joseph.

Jay Strack
Dallas, Texas
Evangelist,
Southern Baptist Convention

1

Heroes or Headhunters?

We **need heroes.** They give us patterns by which we can model our lives. They offer us hope and strength when life seems unfair. We can identify with heroes; they have been where we are and have triumphed. Because of their accomplishments, we feel that we too can make it.

There are different kinds of heroes. Some are good, some are fakes and some are heroes for other reasons. Sometimes people are heroes simply because they outsmart a villain. I am reminded of the Chinese cook who won over some Marines and became a hero.

The cook was the constant source of jokes, and the Marines played trick after trick on him. On one occasion they nailed his shoes to the floor. Another time they welded his pots and pans together. These Marines knew no limit to their pranks. But the remarkable thing was that the cook never got mad. No matter how mean they were to him, he never showed emotion.

One day the soldiers were talking about the cook's incredible patience. Feeling remorse for their jokes and pranks, they decided not to hassle the cook anymore.

They called him to their table in the mess hall and said,

"Cookie, we have done some mean things to you, and we want to say we're sorry. From now on we won't make fun of you or play tricks on you again. You have our word."

"You no more nail shoes to floor?" the cook asked.

"Never again," they replied.

"You never glue pans together with fire gun again?"

"You have our word."

"Okay, I no more spit in soup!"

Who are the heroes?

We all need heroes. Who are yours? Perhaps they are sports figures. Famous youth speaker Tony Campolo talks about his days at West Philadelphia High School. In his school the "jocks" were heroes.

> My high school, West Philadelphia High, . . . was a great school, and I was in the neatest homeroom in the place, Homeroom 48! Homeroom 48 was where the jocks were assigned. And I was a jock.
>
> I want you to know that being a jock is more than simply being athlete. Athletes may play sports, but jocks have style. You can always tell a real jock. A jock doesn't just walk, a jock moves. You have to be cool to be a jock. A jock is the kind of guy who moves down the hallways at school and expects the girls to line up along the walls and sing, "How Great Thou Art."[1]

Many television stars are heroes. I remember attending a youth rally in Orlando with about 300 kids. After one service we were surprised to find 1,500 teenagers lined up outside the convention center. Michael J. Fox was coming to sign autographs later that day.

One of my heroes was the character Rocky, as played by

Sylvester Stalone. I suppose you could say that I was a dedicated Rocky fan. Who could not be encouraged by his story? Here is a second-rate boxer with no future. Then he gets the chance to fight the champion. Though the fight is supposed to be a media show, Rocky takes the opportunity seriously and trains hard. He realizes that he probably cannot win, but he is determined to make a good showing. And he does by almost knocking out the champ. He, the underdog, suddenly is on top.

Oh well . . . so much for Rocky. He can have his smelly gym and punching bags. Real heroes have more to offer than how to get your brains beat out in 10 easy lessons and still look good.

Life is more than winning a fight. Teens today face difficult situations, and they need someone who can give them good advice, someone who can show them how to deal with the trials of growing up.

Real heroes shine in life's hard times. They unselfishly show us what is right. Take Jackie Robinson, for example, the first black person to play major league baseball. In the midst of many racial problems, he stood against the current and brought solutions.

When the manager of the Dodgers contacted him about playing, he told Jackie, "You'll want to quit. Fans will yell at you. Players will call you names from the bench. Pitchers will throw wild balls to hit you in the head. It will be tough, but if you'll gut it out, you'll be a hero."

Jackie Robinson took the challenge, and what a hero he became! He made spectacular hits and incredible catches. In 1947 he was voted Rookie of the Year, and in 1949 he was Most Valuable Player. His batting average at the end of his career was .311. Today, Jackie Robinson is honored in the Baseball Hall of Fame and in the Jackie Robinson Center (Pasadena, California), which was built in 1974 as a memorial to his inspiration to so many black Americans.

Headhunters

Sometimes people who are bold or outspoken are considered heroes. Their willingness to take risks is attractive to timid teens. But having the guts to try the ridiculous does not qualify a person for hero status.

We must choose our heroes carefully. If we follow someone just because we admire his or her abilities or leadership, we may not be following a hero. We may be following a "headhunter."

Headhunters are everywhere. They may be different in appearance, but they promote the same thing—a lifestyle that says whatever feels good, do it, regardless of the consequences. They say things like: "Weekends were made for parties!" "Smoke pot? Sure, don't you?" "If you both have the juices flowing, go for it!" "You got ripped off? Let me help you get even." "If you don't cheat, you must be from another planet." "Just wear a condom. You'll be safe." "You believe in absolutes? Are you a reject from the Mayflower or what?" "Ozzy Osborne rules!" "How will you know something is bad unless you try it?"

One group of headhunters, who are viewed by many teens as heroes, are some of today's secular rock stars. Many openly encourage the use of drugs, sex out of marriage and rebellion against parents and other authority figures. They have completely reversed the meaning of *hero.*

Earlier in this chapter I talked about sports figures being heroes. But selfish individuals out to win at any cost have given the word "competitive" a new meaning. It used to mean clean, honest sportsmanship, but fake heroes have changed its meaning. Steroids and cocaine are as common as Reeboks and warm-up suits. And female competitors in one European country were encouraged to get pregnant six weeks prior to the Olympics and then have an abortion. Why? Because it has been proven medically that women have maximum strength in the sixth week of pregnancy.

Headhunters are not always people, though. Sometimes they are things like alcohol, drugs or sex. After graduation from high school, about 150 of us went to Fort Myers, Florida. We were having a great time swimming and en-

joying the sun and talking about what we were going to do with our lives. Jimmy decided he was going to be a "hero." He got drunk and jumped off the second-floor walkway of the motel into the pool, missing the edge literally by half an inch. He was not a hero. The head-hunter called alcohol almost claimed another victim.

Real heroes

A real hero is someone from whom we can draw strength, courage and inspiration. His or her life is an example that points us to the Hero of heroes, Jesus Christ.

Marie is such a person. She lives in Quito, Ecuador. During spring break one year, our singing group at Toccoa Falls College traveled to Ecuador to give several concerts. They sang in public schools, churches and marketplaces throughout Quito, sharing the love of Jesus.

Following a concert at a high school, one teacher was making fun of the group, saying the members of the group were stupid for believing in Jesus Christ. She said the only thing that was true was humanism and living for yourself. Finally, one person had enough of the teacher's comments.

Marie stood up and spoke out for Jesus. She said she was a Christian and loved God with all her heart. If the teacher would read the Bible, she too would come to love God. When the class saw 95-pound Marie make this stand, other Christian students also began speaking out. As the discussion continued, many non-Christian teens asked questions about Jesus.

When the bell rang at the end of the period, Marie received a standing ovation. Because she was not willing to let the teacher openly mock Jesus, Marie became a hero to her class.

The Bible gives us an example of a real hero, a person who refused to give in to the headhunters of his day — Joseph! If ever there was a candidate for failure, it was Joseph. His family life was horrendous. He was beaten up and shoved around by his half-brothers. His dad was married to four different women — all at the same time! Later, his brothers sold him as a slave, and he was carried off to a foreign country.

Despite the abuse he received and the troubles he experienced, Joseph never gave up on God. Because of his perseverance and his faith in God, Joseph is a hero.

As we look at Joseph's life, be aware of how he handles the different situations that come his way. There will be times when you will say, "That's just what happened to me! I never knew anyone else got hurt like that. I had no idea the Bible talked about people who have been ripped off like this!"

Real heroes are needed for real people and real life. By the time you have finished this study of Joseph, I hope that you will have incorporated into your life some of Joseph's hero qualities.

Steve Camp sings a song called "Where Are The Heroes?" Here are the words:

> Oh we learned of Abraham,
> who was ready to give his son,
> and Noah, who kept on 'til his work was done.
> And Moses led his children safely through the wilderness.
> These men are gone; we're to carry on,

but tell me, why are we in such a mess?
Where are the heroes now, when we need them so
   desperately?
Who will step out from the crowd and be strong
   enough to lead?
Who will teach the children?
Who will show them how?
Oh, I'm asking you, where are the heroes now?

There are those, we don't know their names, who
   were faithful for their Lord.
They were beaten, and they were chained and put to
   death by the sword.
The world was not worthy of them;
is it worthy of me and you?
Oh the saints will endure until the end.
I pray to God that it's true.

We're surrounded by witnesses, as they watch us run
   our race
with our eyes on the author of our faith.
God is not ignorant of the affairs of man and his ways.
Oh He's put us here to make a stand.
He's calling on us today.

He's calling us to be heroes now, when we need them
   so desperately.
Will you step out from the crowd and be strong
   enough to lead?
Will you teach the children?
Will you show them how?
'cause they're asking you, where are the heroes now?

Step out from the crowd.
Step out from the crowd.

Tell me, where are the heroes now?

Taking the challenge
1. Why do people follow leaders?
2. Who are some heroes of today? Why are they heroes?
   Do you agree that they should be heroes?
3. Who are your heroes? Why?
4. What makes a hero a hero according to the definition
   of this chapter?
5. What made Marie a hero?

2
Family Failure

Heritage of the Hero

Often **when we look at heroes,** we wonder what it would be like to live in the spotlight, to walk down the sidewalk and be instantly recognized. Guys might dream of having girls screaming their names and fighting for a chance to touch them. Girls possibly fantasize about being models or movie stars and working in front of a photographer.

We have all dreamed about being a hero, about being admired. But we need to remember that being a hero is not as easy as it looks. In fact, it is often quite difficult. Consider the celebrities and their bodyguards. They also have to maintain an expensive staff to handle bookings, phone calls, appointments and mail. But that is all part of being famous, and it is worth it, right? Well, maybe not.

Elvis Presley, still admired today even though he died in 1977, thought differently about being a star. He was one of the highest paid entertainers in the industry, but he once said that he longed for peace and solitude so much, that he would be willing to pay $1 million to be left alone for one week. All he wanted to do was to be able to walk down the street and not be bothered. That dream never came true.

Heroes become heroes because they are—or were—dedicated individuals. Here is what I mean:

- Those whose names are engraved on the wall of the Vietnam memorial paid the price of dedication to America.
- The track star at your school who holds the record for the mile has his name embossed on a trophy because he did not go home and watch videos and eat buttered popcorn after school. He paid the price of long hours of training and hard work.
- The players on the all-star girls basketball team in your state won because they ran up and down the court until their legs felt like lead and their lungs screamed for relief. They were dedicated to their teammates and to winning.
- Carl Lewis trained 16 years before he had the gold medal hung around his neck at the 1984 Olympics in Los Angeles.
- Abraham Lincoln, one of the best-loved presidents of the United States, paid the price of total commitment. He lost in six attempts at public office, went bankrupt, had a nervous breakdown and buried a son before becoming president.
- People once thought Albert Einstein was retarded, but his persistence in school paid off in great scientific achievements.
- Critics once labeled Vince Lombardi as a person who knew little about football. But by totally dedicating himself to the game, he became a "coach's coach."

Total dedication is the price required to be a hero. Nothing else will work.

Joseph's family

Though a teenager, Joseph was dedicated to God's ways. He may not have understood all that he went through or why he was born into a family plagued with problems. But he trusted God implicitly, believing that He had a purpose for his life. He could have given up, but his persistence paid off.

Joseph's family would have fit in well in our 20th-century America. The Bible describes them as liars, losers, deceivers and murderers. Joseph's father was Jacob, whose name means "deceiver." Jacob certainly lived up to his name. He tricked his father Issac, stealing his brother Esau's birthright. After that, he "hightailed it" to his Uncle Laban's house. While there, Jacob acquired four wives— partly because of the deception of his uncle and partly due to problems compounded by his marriage to two sisters.

Joseph's mother, Rachel, was jealous of her sister, Leah— Jacob's first wife—because she had children and Rachel did not. Because of this, Rachel gave Jacob her servant, Bilhah, to sleep with so that she might become pregnant, thus giving Rachel a child. Bilhah, in effect, became Joseph's third wife. Rachel's actions also got Jacob his fourth wife, Leah's servant.

Rachel was a thief, too. When the Lord told Jacob to leave his uncle's house, Rachel stole some of her father's household belongings. By doing this, she angered her father and deceived Jacob—a crime that could have cost her life had she been found out.

Not only did Joseph grow up in a home with four women trying to be his father's "main woman," but he also had 10 half brothers and one half sister named Dinah.

After leaving his uncle's house and settling in a new land, Jacob's daughter, Dinah, decides to visit the women of the area. A man named Shechem, the son of the ruler of the area, sees her and decides he wants her. So he takes Dinah and rapes her. Her brothers learn of the incident and become angry. They then trick the offender and his father and then murder all the men in Shechem. After that they loot the city and carry off all the women and children.

The story of Joseph's family gets still worse, though. Reuben, Jacob's oldest son, in an effort to establish his rights as the firstborn, sleeps with Bilhah, one of his father's concubines (or as the NIV says, one of Jacob's wives). This act cost Reuben his rights, but more than that, it stigmatized him and Bilhah. Here two family members had sex; incest occurred.

Your family

Putting all this together, we can see that Joseph grew up in a family plagued with problems. Perhaps you can identify with Joseph because your family situation is bad. Perhaps someone in your family has been jailed for deceiving someone or for stealing. Maybe you have been abused—physically or emotionally—by a parent or another relative. When you look at Joseph's background, you say, "He grew up in similar circumstances to what I am growing up in. How in the world did God ever do anything with his life?"

Perhaps you feel that because of your family life God will never be able to use you. Be encouraged! God worked out Joseph's life beyond what anyone could have thought possible, and He can do the same for you. Like Joseph's, your portrait can hang in the Hall of Heroes.

But you have to be willing to *let* God use you. You have to turn the hurt over to Him. You have to lay before Him those misunderstandings and that deep family secret that haunts you. You have to allow Him to alter your life, to break up those patterns established from the poor role models in your life.

He can handle that painful childhood memory. Let Him. If He could be there for Joseph and reshape him, surely He can do the same for you too. He enjoys setting people free.

Why not pray this prayer:

> Lord Jesus, I need to be set free from some things that are part of my heritage. Because You are faithful today, as You were for Joseph in his day, I want to unload all of this trash and let You do with it as You wish. Jesus, I lay _____, _____ and _____ at Your feet. No longer will I be chained to those things. Starting today, I determine that I will be different by Your power. Thank You, Lord. I'm yours and I'm free!

Taking the challenge

1. What are some hazards of being a hero?
2. How does dedication fit into being a hero?
3. How was Joseph dedicated to the Lord's ways despite a poor home situation?
4. Name some of the problems in Joseph's immediate family.
5. Can you see any similarities in your family?
6. Did you pray the prayer at the end of the chapter? Do you feel hopeful? Why or why not?

3

Birth Order

Downfall of the Hero

Have you ever wondered why the youngest brother or sister in a family seems to be able to get away with murder? Amazingly, the oldest always seems to be treated as though he or she is in boot camp. But when the youngest arrives on the scene, he or she is always regarded as "the baby." We hear things like: "Stop hitting your baby brother." "You have to baby-sit your little sister tonight." "Don't make the baby cry."

And what about this scenario: you tell your younger brother not to ride his bicycle in the street or to stop sticking his finger in the electrical sockets. Then he runs, with crocodile tears in his eyes, to your parents screaming that you were mean to him. You end up being grounded until you're 23!

In recent years much research has been done on the birth order and how it affects people. A leading Christian psychologist, Dr. Kevin Lehman, has discovered the following characteristics among the various orders of birth:

Oldest Child—perfectionist, reliable, conscientious, list-maker, well organized, critical, serious, scholarly.

Middle Child — mediator, least amount of photographs in the family album, avoids conflicts, independent, extreme loyalty to peer group, many friends, a maverick.

Youngest Child — manipulative, charming, blames others, shows off, people person, good salesperson, precocious, engaging.[2]

There you have it! The youngest can get away with incredible things, while Mom and Dad smile and say,

"Isn't little Joey precious?" "Doesn't Sally know a lot for her age?"

This helps us understand why Joseph was so special to his father, Jacob – and why his brothers ended up hating him. Remember the account in Genesis when Jacob was about to meet his brother Esau after years of separation? Jacob took Joseph and put him in the *back* of the procession.

> Jacob looked up and there was Esau, coming with his four hundred men; so he divided the children among Leah, Rachel and the two maidservants. He put the maidservants and their children in front, Leah and her children next, and Rachel and Joseph in the rear. (Genesis 33:1–2)

Why did Jacob do that? For one reason – Joseph was his favorite, and he wanted to protect him from a possible bloody confrontation with Esau. Notice what Genesis 37:3 says: "Now Israel [Jacob] loved Joseph more than any of his other sons, because he had been born to him in his old age."

But before we slice young Joseph to bits because he was loved by Jacob, perhaps we should look closer into Joseph's relationship with his father. Genesis 37:2 sheds some light here:

> This is the account of Jacob.
>
> Joseph, a young man of seventeen, was tending the flocks with his brothers, the sons of Bilhah and the sons of Zilpah, his father's wives, and he brought their father a bad report about them.

When I first read this, I said to myself, "What a nerd!

What kind of wimp is this guy Joseph anyway? He's nothing but a tattletale." I was even more confused as I read further in verses 4–11:

> When his brothers saw that their father loved him more than any of them, they hated him and could not speak a kind word to him.
>
> Joseph had a dream, and when he told it to his brothers, they hated him all the more. He said to them, "Listen to this dream I had: We were binding sheaves of grain out in the field when suddenly my sheaf rose and stood upright, while your sheaves gathered around mine and bowed down to it."
>
> His brothers said to him, "Do you intend to reign over us? Will you actually rule us?" And they hated him all the more because of his dream and what he had said.
>
> Then he had another dream, and he told it to his brothers. "Listen," he said, "I have had another dream, and this time the sun and moon and eleven stars were bowing down to me."
>
> When he told his father as well as his brothers, his father rebuked him and said, "What is this dream you had? Will your mother and I and your brothers actually come and bow down to the ground before you?" His brothers were jealous of him, but his father kept the matter in mind.

In studying and thinking this through I have seen that my first reaction was not right. Joseph had nothing to do with his birth order. He could not help how his father felt about him. Nor could he change the fact that he had the dreams. He told the truth. The same applies to the time he told Jacob about the wrongs his brothers had done. He did not invent the evils; he reacted to them in truth. Frankly, I began to admire Joseph for that. Honesty was a virtue that was lacking in Joseph's family.

God's call to us: Stand against the wrong!

We need to follow Joseph's example and take a stand. Scripture tells us that as redeemed children of God, we are to oppose sin. The decision to do that is hard, but it is worth it. I remember when I was forced to take a stand for God's truth. The occasion was a reunion with old friends at a Pizza Hut.

Andy, Sam and I were close friends in high school. We hung around together in the cafeteria and on the ball field, and we often arranged our schedules so that we could be in the same classes. We never dated a girl unless the other two approved, and we even triple-dated to the prom!

In my senior year of high school, I began to sense that God was calling me to go 100 percent for Him, so I made the decision to attend a Bible college. And so I did. When I came home for Christmas break that first year, I telephoned Andy and Sam. We decided to get together for a pizza.

When we got to Pizza Hut, we reminisced about old times. Then the waitress came. Suddenly I was put on the defensive. The conversation went like this:

> Sam: "We'll take two large super supremes and a pitcher of Budweiser with three mugs."
> Me: "Uh, no thanks, I'll just have a coke."
> Andy: "What's the matter with you? You aren't still

excited about this Jesus thing are you?"

Sam: "Yeah, Les, come on. You can have just one beer. I mean one lousy beer—big deal."

Me: "Look you guys, I appreciate your offer, but drinking is against my convictions. Thanks anyway."

Sam: "Les, either have a beer or just start walkin' home. What's it gonna be?"

Andy: "Wait a minute, Sam. If he doesn't want to drink, he doesn't want to drink. Give him a break."

The pizzas and the beer and my coke came, but I had lost my appetite. I nibbled at a piece or two and tried to remain calm. Our conversation was limited, and when they took me home, I knew our friendship was over.

That night, I knelt beside my bed trying to pray, but all I could do was weep for my friends. I felt so betrayed. But at the same time I was joyful. My stand for God's truth was more important than anything in the world—more important than sports, more important than being cool in front of others and more important than my best friends.

To this day, I have not heard from Andy or Sam. Andy moved out of town and left no forwarding address. I do not know what happened to Sam. I do know this, though: Jesus is a friend who sticks closer than a brother, and He offers truth to those who seek it.

Joseph stood up for truth. He was not a wimp or a chump. He was a teenager with guts!

I am glad I stood up for God's ways. He is calling others to do the same, especially today when dishonesty and corruption seem to rule in government, business and even supposedly Christian enterprises.

John Wesley, founder of the Methodist churches, once

said, "Give me three hundred men who fear nothing but God, hate nothing but sin, and are determined to serve God, and I will set the world on fire for God."

I believe God is calling some teens to answer Wesley's challenge – to love God, to hate sin and to be determined to go God's way regardless of what happens.

Joseph was determined to stand for the truth. We will see more of his determination in later chapters. There needs to be an army of teenage Josephs today who are willing to stand for God's values. God is looking for people who fear nothing but Him, hate nothing but sin and want nothing short of His best.

Regardless of our human birth order, Jesus has given us a new order of birth. As His born-again children, our duty is to oppose evil and stand up for truth.

Taking the challenge

1. What do you think of Dr. Lehman's research on the oldest, middle and youngest child?
2. Have you ever felt that one of your brothers or sisters was favored over you? Why?
3. Joseph was a teen who stood up for truth. How can his life apply to yours?

4

Family Feud

Banishment of the Hero

Have you ever had a family fight? Stupid question, right? Squabbles and disagreements are a normal part of family life.

I remember a fight my brother Buck and I had. He wore my good shoes to a New Year's Eve party without asking me. But that was not the worse part of it. I was going to church that night and had no shoes to wear. I ended up wearing my old sneakers, the ones that I mowed the grass in. I was so mad that I put 25 sandspurs in his bed. I woke up later that night to his complaints: "Ouch, there's another one!" I rolled over and went back to sleep with a big smile on my face. "Mission accomplished!"

Sometimes family fights are more serious than my getting even with my brother. Chuck Swindoll tells a story about two unmarried sisters who lived together. Something serious had come between them that caused a fight. They ended up marking a white line down the middle of their small cottage separating one's side from the other's. For years the two did not cross into each other's territory. They did eat at the same table, but they never spoke. Now that is a family fight![3]

On a recent newscast, I heard about a 14-year-old boy

who got mad at his family. He was so angry that he took a 12-gauge shotgun and killed his baby-sitter, his mother and father and then himself.

"Done in" by his brothers

Joseph experienced what could be termed the ultimate

family feud. At this point in his life, Joseph's brothers despise him because of their father's feelings toward him. In Genesis 37 we read:

> So Joseph went after his brothers and found them near Dothan. But they saw him in the distance, and before he reached them, they plotted to kill him.
> "Here comes that dreamer!" they said to each other. "Come now, let's kill him and throw him into one of these cisterns and say that a ferocious animal devoured him. Then we'll see what becomes of his dreams." (verses 17–20)

As the narrative continues we learn that Reuben prevents the other brothers from killing Joseph; Reuben had a plan to rescue Joseph and return him safely to his father. But when Reuben is away, a group of traders happen by, and the brothers decide to sell Joseph as a slave. Scripture then tells us that the traders take Joseph to Egypt and sell him to Potiphar.

Protecting family members is one of the first laws of society, but here we find family members willing to kill one of their own—and they would have killed Joseph except for Reuben's intervention. Instead they do the next worse thing, they sell Joseph as a slave to a group of foreign merchants. They were consumed by their hatred for their brother. One wonders how they slept that night.

"Traded off" cheaply

In today's society children and teenagers are "traded off" cheaply—not exactly as Joseph was traded off, but the effects are the same. Sometimes teens are discarded simply by what their parents say, or more often, what is not said. Sometimes it happens because parents are too busy. Their families end up being pushed aside, ignored. No matter how it happens, though, the "trade off" hurts.

Angie sat in my office one day, tearfully describing something that happened to her. A close, trusted relative forced her into having sex with him. She sobbed for over an hour, repeating again and again, "I trusted him so much. How could he have taken such advantage of me?"

I cried with Angie. Her trust had been abused by some unthinking, uncaring clod, bent only on his own selfish satisfaction.

A few years ago, I heard a story about a young woman who fell in love with a young man who was called to the mission field. He was accepted by a mission board and assigned to China. The two planned for Jim to travel on to China, become established and then send for Janet. They would marry in China.

Janet's childhood dream was to be a missionary to China. Now the dream seemed to be coming true. She was on cloud nine.

Jim left for China. Month after month passed, and every day Janet expected a letter from him. Fourteen months passed and still no letter.

Finally, two and a half years later, she heard from China, but the news was not what she had waited for—Jim had married another woman.

Janet was devastated. She wept for months, rarely coming out of her room. She would not see anyone. Bitterness consumed her life. Janet never married and spent her time taking care of her aging mother.

Shortly after her mother's death, Janet was in the attic of their house going through her mother's things. While sorting through some old papers, she found a stack of letters. Guess where they were from? China! All were addressed to Janet, but none of them had been opened.

Janet was shocked. As she carefully opened one, she found tickets for her passage to China. Jim had been faithful, but Janet's mother had intercepted the correspondence. Why? Evidently she could not bear the thought of her daughter living so far away. Janet never knew about the letters until it was 40 years too late.

Have you been sold short?

Perhaps you, like Joseph and Janet, have been sold short by your family. You may ache so deeply that you have considered running away and never letting your family hear from you again. Maybe you have thought about suicide.

If you are trapped in an emotional prison, I have good news for you. The Lord has the keys to unlock the door to that cage. Jesus was rejected and forgotten about, too. Like Joseph, He was sold for silver—His honesty, compassion and love were denied for 30 pieces of silver. Jesus knows how you feel, and He is there when you need Him.

Ken found that out. He attends Campus Church at Toccoa Falls College where I am the pastor. His is a powerful story.

Ken was 25 years old, the owner of a successful construction business in Atlanta. His company was building 45 houses a year. He drove a new Ford Bronco, complete with mobile phone, and lived in a $250,000 home. It was a common thing for him to deposit $100,000 in his checking account. He thought he had it made.

But then Ken found Jesus Christ as his Lord and Savior.

Family Feud

When his business partner of five years learned that Ken had decided to serve the Lord 100 percent, he became angry. He tried to entice Ken away from God by telling him he could be a millionaire in three years. When Ken refused he swore he would see to it that Ken's business would be "belly-up" in three months.

Ken stuck to his commitment to Christ, and just as the crooked partner had promised, Ken was out of business in three months—completely broke.

As Ken and I talked over coffee, I asked him how it felt to have someone he trusted kick him in the teeth for a few lousy bucks.

"I ached so bad I didn't think I could take anymore," he said. "But I knew the Lord was with me. The thing I remember most, however, is the joy my wife and I felt as we drove up to start school at Toccoa Falls College. No matter what man had done to us, Jesus was still with us. We had to pull off the road because we were weeping with the joy of His presence."

Jesus was there for Ken when he was sold out, and He is there for you.

Taking the challenge
1. What are your family fights about?
2. Have you ever been rejected? How did it feel?
3. Who do you know that has been shoved around by life, family or friends? What can you do to help?
4. What would you do if your parents intercepted your mail?
5. What would you have done if you were Ken and your business partner did what his did?

5

Potiphar's Wife

Temptation of the Hero

This may be a shocker to some people, but women were liberated before women's lib. They were "self-sufficient" before Jane Fonda produced her first video or Gloria Steinem led women across America in burning their bras. Women were "freed" before receiving the right to vote. Their "liberation" was initiated before they were permitted to smoke cigarettes, do the Charleston and wear pants. Women were "unyoked" even before the founding of America. If we were to study the subject, our research would take us back to the days of the pyramids.

Egyptologists tell that Egyptian women were liberated. In fact, compared to our day and time, they were "super-liberated." Wow!

Joseph grew into his early 20s in this setting. He was a normal 20-year-old male. Yet the amazing thing about Joseph is that when temptation came, he was above average in his response. What a model to follow!

Temptation is powerful, and it comes in many forms. Mouthing off is one form. So is trying to impress people. Cheating is another temptation as are drinking and drugs. But one of the strongest temptations for teens is sex.

Josh McDowell tells about a 14-year-old girl who got caught in the sex crunch.

When I was only fourteen years of age, I dated an eighteen-year-old boy. After a month or so of dating, he told me that he loved me and had to "have me." He said that if I loved him, I would have sex with him.

And if I wouldn't, he couldn't control his desire for me and would have to break up with me.

What did I think at fourteen years of age? I knew sex was wrong before marriage, and I didn't want to lose my virginity. And yet I so desired to have a man love me . . . so I finally gave in.

I felt so guilty afterward. I can remember sobbing in my bed at night after I'd come home from being with my boyfriend. I wanted so much to have my virginity back. And yet it was gone, forever. My self-esteem certainly didn't improve, but worsened, and I needed my boyfriend's love more than ever. I began to feel so lonely inside, and yet there was no one I could turn to. Certainly not my father, who would really "hate" me if he ever knew what an awful thing I had done.

Well, after two years, I broke up with my boyfriend, but soon had another, and went through the same cycle with him. And then with another. Was I any more secure with myself? No, I was a puppet in any man's hands, for I wanted so desperately to find someone who would love me unconditionally.

Isn't that ironic? The very thing I searched for— unconditional love—was being offered to me conditionally. "If you love me, you'll do it."[4]

How to avoid the temptation trap

Avoiding the temptation trap is not something teens learn in school. The NBC evening news with Tom Brokaw will never announce temptation's defeat. Phil Donahue will never interview a guest who has invented a vaccine that prevents temptation. Mike Tyson may have knocked out Leon Spinks with a few punches, but physical strength will not bring temptation down for the count.

Temptation cannot be defeated *naturally* – it takes *super-* natural strength. Joseph discovered this when Potiphar's wife repeatedly tried to seduce him.

Think about it. Here is Joseph in his early 20s. He is not a freak; he is a normal guy with normal desires. He is a foreigner in a country known for its liberated women, and he is lonely and has never been on a date.

In addition to this, Joseph is a slave. He has been sold as if he were a bull at the livestock yard. He is then forced to do whatever his master bids him to do. Can you imagine Joseph taking this treatment after living like royalty in his father's house?

But Joseph made the best of the situation. He believed that the Lord was with him, and he made up his mind to be the best slave he could be. Scripture says that

> The Lord was with Joseph and he prospered, and he lived in the house of his Egyptian master. When his master saw that the Lord was with him and that the Lord gave him success in everything he did, Joseph found favor in his eyes and became his attendant. Potiphar put him in charge of his household, and he entrusted to his care everything he owned. From the time he put him in charge of his household and of all that he owned, the Lord blessed the household of the Egyptian because of Joseph. The blessing of the Lord was on everything Potiphar had, both in the house and in the field. So he left in Joseph's care everything he had; with Joseph in charge, he did not concern himself with anything except the food he ate. (Genesis 39:3–6)

Joseph's hard work worked for Potiphar. Potiphar advanced himself when he advanced Joseph. And Mrs. Potiphar could not have been more delighted. Giving Joseph more responsibility freed up Potiphar to spend more time at the Cairo Country Club, improving his golf game and working on his tan.

Meanwhile, Mrs. Potiphar was working on her own game plan – figuring out a way to lure Joseph into her bed. She was not about to take no for an answer. Why should she? She was the master's wife, and she got what she wanted. And she wanted Joseph. "Now Joseph was well-built and handsome, and after a while his master's wife took notice of Joseph and said, 'Come to bed with me'" (Genesis 39:6–7).

Joseph's response is incredible. He could have followed through on an offer that must have seemed like a dream, yet he saw the potential nightmare it would be in reality. Notice his keen insight into what was real and what would have been a wreck.

> But he refused. "With me in charge," he told her, "my master does not concern himself with anything in the house; everything he owns he has entrusted to my care. No one is greater in this house than I am. My master has withheld nothing from me except you, because you are his wife. How then could I do such a wicked thing and sin against God?" (Genesis 39:8–9)

Joseph immediately refused her advances and that is important. Suppressing the first desire is easier than satisfying all that follow it. Sometimes, however, a constant chipping away at something can cause an avalanche. Apparently that was Mrs. Potiphar's strategy, for the next verse reads, "And though she spoke to Joseph day after day . . ." (Genesis 39:10).

How did Joseph stand against this onslaught? What kept him from succumbing to her suggestive ideas and soft voice? I am convinced that it was a supernatural infusion from the Lord. The proof is in Genesis 39:2: "The Lord was with Joseph."

Avoiding the "baited hook"

The same is true for us. When temptation comes our way, we have to refuse. It may look luscious and gratifying and inviting, but so is a piece of bait to a fish. What the fish does not see is the hook that will eventually haul it to the dinner table.

I grew up in Fort Myers, Florida. My family and I often fished off of Sanibel Island and Captiva Pass, usually with great success.

Once when I was 10 years old, I was with my dad and brother out in the Gulf of Mexico. As I baited the hook, I hesitantly threw my line in the water. Within three minutes, I had hooked a fish and, as I soon found out, was in for the toughest fight I had ever had!

My dad saw how the rod was bending and how I was reeling as hard as I could. He grabbed a net as I fought with all my might to land what I thought was a whale. I got it up to the boat, and my dad made a swoop for it with the net. Just then the fish dove for the bottom. I kept fighting until my arms ached and I could barely reel anymore. Finally, I got the fish in close enough to the boat for Dad to scoop it up in the net. It was a 17-inch mangrove snapper. In 40 years of fishing those waters, my father had never seen one that big. He was so pleased he had it mounted for me. What a prize it is even today, some 20 years later.

How did I catch that snapper? By baiting the hook. The fish saw the bait and snapped. The problem was not the bait, it was the hook! The result? The fish is on my office wall.

The same is true with temptation. The book of James tells us this:

> When tempted, no one should say, "God is tempting me." For God cannot be tempted by evil, nor does he tempt anyone; but each one is tempted when, by his own desire, he is dragged away and enticed. Then, after desire has conceived, it gives birth to sin; and sin, when it is full-grown, gives birth to death. (James 1:13–16)

The temptation is held out before us. We do not *have* to strike at the bait, but if we do, we lose—every time.

Mrs. Potiphar "dangled the bait" in front of Joseph, promising him satisfaction and fulfillment. No longer would he have to be lonely.

Yet Joseph refused. He knew God was with him and that God's ways were higher than the emotional zing of being with a woman who enticed him to sin. Right on, Joseph! What a hero!

You—a winner over temptation

When temptation comes, we too can win over it. Notice I said "when." Temptation *will* appear, no question about that. But we do not have to fall for its sucker punch. We can refuse, even as Joseph did. When we apply the truths in God's Word, we win. Here is the plan:

1. *Acknowledge His presence.* Christ promises to be with us when temptation to sin comes.

> And surely I am with you always, to the very end of the age. (Matthew 28:20)

> Never will I leave you;
>   never will I forsake you. (Hebrews 13:5)

> Where can I go from your Spirit?
>   Where can I flee from your presence? (Psalm 139:7)

2. *Claim His power.* Not only did Christ assure us of His presence, but He said that He would provide power for us to overcome temptation.

> For everyone born of God overcomes the world. This is the victory that has overcome the world, even our faith. Who is it that overcomes the world? Only he who believes that Jesus is the Son of God. (1 John 5:4–5)

> You, dear children, are from God and have overcome them, because the one who is in you is greater that the one who is in the world. (1 John 4:4)

> But a time is coming, and has come, when you will be scattered, each to his own home. You will leave me all alone. Yet I am not alone, for my Father is with me. (John 16:32)

> I can do everything through him who gives me strength. (Philippians 4:13)

3. *Do not let past failures keep defeating you.* God knows about your failures, and He has made a way for you to be cleansed and forgiven. When you apply what He says, you are a victor!

> My dear children, I write this to you so that you will not sin. But if anybody does sin, we have one who speaks to the Father in our defense—Jesus Christ, the Righteous One.

> I write to you, dear children,
>> because your sins have been forgiven on account of his name. (1 John 2:1, 12)

We *can* overcome temptation. We do not have to bite the bait.

More than words

In a remote part of the Amazon jungle, there is a tribe of people where the women are demanding of their potential husbands. They want more than a smiling face whispering, "I love you."

The men must thrust their hands into straw mittens that are filled with stinger insects. A bite from one of these bugs can make the human hand swell to twice its normal size.

But that is not the tough part. Bells are tied around the knees of the men. If they flinch enough to ring the bells, the wedding is off!

God is looking for people who have more to offer than words. He is looking for men and women who will not flinch when the sin of the world delivers its alluring venom. He is looking for hearts that swell with a love devotion to His ways. That is the kind of person Joseph was. Even though his body screamed out for sexual gratification, his love for God overruled his desires. What a hero!

How about you? Is God calling you to be His hero? If you have tried and failed, He will help you start over again. With His help, you can win over temptation.

Alice discovered this to be true. She was ashamed at giving in to having sex with her boyfriend. She saw herself as a defeated person. As I shared God's plan with her, she fought back the tears. Could this be her answer? Yes! A few days later, she wrote me this note:

> Last week when I was home for spring break, I was really asking the Lord to guard me from sinning against Him with Jim. He assured me that if I was willing to go His way I would win. Sure enough, His ways proved true. Though temptation was knocking on the door good and loud, by the power of Christ in me, I refused to open. In Christ, I won!

Alice experienced the same power in her life that Joseph experienced in his. As we follow God's plan of acknowledging His will, claiming His power and not letting past failures defeat us, we too can be set free!

Taking the challenge

1. Describe some ways that women are liberated today.
2. How did you react to the 14-year-old girl's story? Was she tempted beyond what you have been? If you could talk with her, what would you say?
3. Describe what is meant by fighting temptation supernaturally.

4. What would you do if you were Joseph and Mrs. Potiphar began to "put the moves on you"? Has something like that ever happened to you? If so, what did you do? Are you happy about the way you reacted? Why or why not?

5. Can we be certain that temptation will come? What can we do when it does?

6. Write out the three things we can do when the bait of temptation is dropped in front of us.

7. Lay out a specific plan using these three things when temptation comes your way in the form of lying, cheating, mouthing off, sex and rebellion.

6
Rumors & Lies

Exploitation of the Hero

Rumors hurt. So do lies. They can have devastating effects on a person. A family in North Dakota found this out the hard way.

We could have classified this family as an "all-American" family. They were well thought of in their community. Every day when the father came home from work, his wife and two children would greet him at the door and shower him with hugs and kisses. Things were going great for them.

Then someone started a nasty rumor about the man, saying he was cheating on his wife. Though the rumor was completely untrue, it persisted. The once-happy marriage began to disintegrate.

One day the husband came home from work to a silent house. No one greeted him at the door. He walked in and called out. No one answered. He walked through the house, looking everywhere. Nothing. For some reason he decided to look in the basement. What he saw floored him. Hanging from a rafter were his two children and wife. Unable to cope with the rumors any longer, she had killed the children and herself.

A man in Georgia experienced the same kind of thing.
Douglas Forbes was on his usual evening walk one night.
In an area of town near where he lived, two women were
raped. Forbes, being dressed in clothes similar to the assailant, was arrested and charged with the rapes. His
picture was in every newspaper in Georgia. Rumors circu-
lated. Both of the women identified him as their assailant,
and he was convicted and sentenced to 60 years in
prison.

His wife had to sell everything the family possessed to
pay the legal bills and meet the family's financial needs.
Eventually she took a job as a waitress. Forbes's 16-year-

old daughter, destined for a great career in track, was forced to quit the team to work after school.

Forbes served five years and would have served longer, but the real rapist was captured and confessed to the earlier crimes. Forbes became a victim of rumors and false accusations.

Joseph—victim

Most of us have been subjected to rumors and lies, and while their effects are usually not as disastrous as the examples cited above, they can still be serious. I remember once in ninth grade being the victim of rumors. The worst part was that I was 2,500 miles away and could not defend myself.

I had flown from Florida to Vermont to work for my brother for the summer. About midway through July, I received a letter from my girlfriend telling me about some things another boy had told her about me. He, of course, wanted her to be his girlfriend and saw a chance to make me look bad while I was away. In the closing paragraph she said I could go shoot marbles on the interstate for all she cared!

Joseph experienced the effects of rumors and lies. When he refused Potiphar's wife's advances, she became angry, angry enough to invent a lie about Joseph. She said that Joseph had tried to rape her. What was the result of her lie?

When his master heard the story his wife told him, saying, "This is how your slave treated me," he burned with anger. Joseph's master took him and put him in prison, the place where the king's prisoners were confined. (Genesis 39:19–20)

Can you imagine how Joseph must have felt? He had been true to God and his master. He had run from sin, but what had it gotten him? Imprisonment! Here he was in jail, falsely accused. Why was God allowing this to happen?

Many of us have experienced the same kind of treatment. The explosive shrapnel of false stories has wounded even the most respected teens. The lie that Karla was sleeping with her boyfriend wiped out her Christian testimony. Alan lost the respect of his coaches and teammates when someone started a rumor that he had cheated on final exams. Alice became a social outcast after someone said she had attempted suicide twice during her sophomore year. She did not have a date in 14 months because of that lie.

God is with us

Like Joseph we wonder why such things happen to us. But God was with Joseph, and He is with us too. "But while Joseph was there in the prison, the Lord was with him; he showed him kindness and granted him favor in the eyes of the prison warden" (Genesis 39:21).

The apostle Paul knew about the hardships caused by lies and rumors. Notice what he wrote when lies had caused him problems.

> Praise be to the God and Father of our Lord Jesus Christ, the Father of compassion and the God of all comfort, who comforts us in all our troubles, so that we can comfort those in any trouble with the comfort

we ourselves have received from God. For just as the sufferings of Christ flow over into our lives, so also through Christ our comfort overflows. If we are distressed, it is for your comfort and salvation; if we are comforted, it is for your comfort, which produces in you patient endurance of the same sufferings we suffer. And our hope for you is firm, because we know that just as you share in our sufferings, so also you share in our comfort. (2 Corinthians 1:3–7)

Did you get that? God can bring His people through the pain of rumors and lies. Dr. Helen Rosevere can attest to that.

Dr. Rosevere was a medical missionary in Africa for many years. During her first term on the field she set up a hospital, working side-by-side with the nationals in pouring the cement floor, building the walls, putting on the roof and painting the inside. After the hospital was built, she started her medical ministry. Countless times she went out in the middle of the night to deliver babies, perform emergency surgery or help distressed Africans. She was totally committed to the people.

Then the political situation in the country changed. Rumors began to circulate, describing white people as evil and against blacks. Unrest swept through the towns and villages where Dr. Rosevere worked.

Late one night, several men broke into her house. In a matter of minutes, they destroyed 30 years of work and research. Then the men beat up Dr. Rosevere and raped her.

Numb with pain, she could not understand why this had happened. She had given herself totally to the people, and now this. The only thing she could do was to lay herself before the Lord and weep.

God took Helen Rosevere's pain and questions and hurts and restored her to full-time ministry. The work to which she had dedicated her life was restored and even increased. God proved to her, as He did to Joseph, that He is bigger than rumors and lies.

Is it possible that you, like the man in North Dakota and Joseph, have been lied about? Maybe you have been in a "dungeon of despair" because of devastating rumors. Will you begin today to let God work in that situation? Allow Him to unlock the door of discouragement that has confined you for so long. He will relieve the hurts and heal the wounds you have received from the shrapnel of rumors.

Taking the challenge

1. What is the worst part of lies and rumors?
2. How did you react to the story about the North Dakota family? What would you say to the 16-year-old daughter of the man falsely accused of rape?
3. Have you ever been lied about? What happened? What did you do about it?
4. Have you ever told a lie or spread a rumor about someone else? Did they ever find out about it? If so, how did it make you feel?
5. If you could write a one-page article about rumors and lies, what are some things you would include?
6. Imagine you are Joseph. You have been honest and loyal. Mrs. Potiphar lies about you and you are thrown into jail. What would you say to the Lord?

7

Friends

Betrayal of the Hero

When people get mad, they do incredible things. They cuss, spit, cry, get quiet, shake with anger or look for the nearest dog to kick or door to slam. Many times, they look for ways to get even.

A woman died, leaving in her will $1.00 to her husband. The reason? She hoped he would buy a rope and hang himself!

A bank in Marin County, California, made an appeal to new customers to open a checking account. Bring a personal photograph, they said, and they would print it free on the first group of checks. A divorced man decided to respond to the offer. When the checks arrived, he used the account to make alimony payments to his first wife. The photo he had printed in the background was of him passionately kissing his second wife!

Forgotten by a friend

If ever there was a person who could have been vengeful, it was Joseph. He has grown up in a family plagued by problems. His half brothers despised him and would have killed him except that something better came along—they sold him into slavery. Joseph was then carried off to a foreign country and sold again. Just when things were looking up, the rug was snatched out from under him, and he finds himself in jail because of lies.

But he has not hit bottom yet. In prison he makes friends with a couple of Pharaoh's servants who had lost their master's favor. Joseph treats them kindly and at one point when they both have strange dreams, Joseph tells them what they mean. The cupbearer promises to remember Joseph when he is released from prison and restored to his place in Pharaoh's court.

Does the man keep his word? Scripture tells us that "The chief cupbearer, . . . did not remember Joseph; he forgot him" (Genesis 40:23). This could have been the last straw for Joseph. A person he thought was his friend forgets him. Has this ever happened to you? It happened to Kevin.

Kevin and Jeff were best friends. They camped out together on weekends, double-dated to school dances and always hung out together at school. Their sophomore year, one would not join the wrestling team unless the other did. They were as close as two friends could be. Their future plans included getting an apartment together after graduation from high school. Then came the summer of their junior year.

Kevin decided to work with his family instead of at the summer job that he and Jeff had planned to do together. Although Kevin did not intend to hurt his friend, Jeff was crushed. He refused to speak to Kevin after that. When school started the next September, Jeff dropped the courses that he and Kevin had signed up for. Kevin repeatedly tried to rebuild the relationship, but Jeff would have nothing to do with him.

Friends

Carolyn knows what it means to be rejected by a friend, too. Carolyn and Judy were close friends. They worked together in children's ministries and youth groups in school. Every summer they worked at a teen camp they had organized. They had unlimited potential for reaching other teens for Christ. They were on the move for God!

Then something happened to Judy. She seemed distracted much of the time, and the two began to drift apart. While at a weekend retreat, Carolyn noticed that Judy was uneasy during a message. When the invitation to respond was given, Judy ran to the altar and wept like a baby. Carolyn followed her. Between sobs, she told Carolyn she had gotten involved with a married man. After the retreat he was coming to get her on his motorcycle. They planned to live together.

Judy was miserable with her sin and wanted out of the commitment. As Judy and Carolyn prayed that evening, they wept together and asked for God's forgiveness. They prayed that Judy would be strong enough the next day to tell her boyfriend that she was not going with him. When they went to their room, Judy felt at peace. Her decision to serve the Lord was firm, and her friendship with Carolyn was restored.

About 3:00 the next afternoon, Judy's boyfriend arrived as planned. Carolyn watched from a distance as Judy went out to meet him. The minutes passed into a half hour as Judy and the man discussed the matter. All Carolyn could do was pray. Then the unthinkable happened— Judy climbed on the motorcycle and the two rode away.

Judy had decided that her relationship with the Lord and her friendship with Carolyn were no longer important. Carolyn was crushed. She felt alone and betrayed, and she ached for her friend. Her emotions switched back and forth from anger to sadness, and she wondered if she would ever be normal again.

Unlocking the doors of despair

How do we climb out of the dungeons of despair after we have been ripped off? What did Joseph do? Did he make up a blacklist of all the people he wanted to get even with? Did he kick the doors of his cell or scream loud enough to wake the dead? No. Never once does Scripture record that Joseph became bitter. He continued

to believe that the sovereign God had a plan for his life.

That was the key that unlocked the dungeon door for Joseph, and it can be the key that unlocks the door to the hurts that have chained us. When we understand that God is with us always (Hebrews 13:5), we find remarkable strength to press on.

Notice what the Bible says:

> Humble yourselves, therefore, under God's mighty hand, that he may lift you up in due time. Cast all your anxiety on him because he cares for you. (1 Peter 5:6–7)

> Be still, and know that I am God;
>   I will be exalted among the nations,
>   I will be exalted in the earth. (Psalm 46:10)

God's presence is greater than problems. Joseph found that out. So did Carolyn. Today, despite the deep wound left from seeing Judy ride off on that motorcycle, Carolyn is still speaking at camps and encouraging teens to live for Jesus.

Your blacklists

What are you going to do with your blacklists? Realistically, you only have two options. You can harbor hate, bitterness and anger in your life, or you can be set free.

Corrie ten Boom is famous for her stand for God during her time spent in a Nazi prison camp. Forgiving her captors was not an easy thing for her to do, but she knew it was the only way for her to be set free.

Corrie was sent to prison for helping Jewish people

escape from Hitler's army. While there she suffered horribly. Solitary confinement seemed to last a lifetime. She was bitter cold in the winter and barely survived the sweltering heat of summer. She saw her father and sister die in the camp.

I heard her describe her most humiliating experience. Every Friday the women of the camp were forced to undress and parade naked past the German guards and their groping hands and jeering voices.

While speaking at a conference many years after her imprisonment, she noticed a man standing in the back of the room. She vaguely recognized his face. After Corrie finished speaking, the man came up to her and stuck out his hand saying, "I am a Christian now, too." Suddenly it dawned on her who he was—one of her former prison guards.

She hesitated to take his hand. Here was a man who had been partly responsible for the death of her father and sister as well as for much of her own pain and suffering. By God's grace, though, Corrie was able to take the man's hand and accept him as a brother in Christ.

How did that happen? The same way it did for Joseph, Carolyn and many others. They all refused to allow bitterness to grow in their lives. Instead they allowed the Lord to unlock the door of their dungeon of despair.

Just as God was with Joseph in that cold, damp jail cell, enabling him to continue on, so He is with you in that dark, cold corner where you have been bruised, hurt and rejected. You can be set free. Though it is a brave step, God's presence is there for you. Dare to believe Him today. "If the Son sets you free, you will be free indeed" (John 8:36).

Taking the challenge

1. What are some things for which people make black-lists, hold a grudge or want to get even?
2. Have you ever been really mad? About what?
3. As you think about Joseph's life, how do you think you would have reacted?
4. Have you ever been rejected like Carolyn and Kevin were? What did you do about it?
5. Hebrews 13:5 says, "Never will I leave you;/ never will I forsake you." Do you believe that?
6. Make a banner that has the verse found in John 8:36 written on it. Hang it on your bedroom wall.

8

Dreams

Deliverance of the Hero

I **will never forget March 1987.** I had been riding for
seven days on a Greyhound bus with the touring choir of
Toccoa Falls College, and I was depressed. We had been in
a number of churches, singing every night. I had been
sick the whole time, and what made matters worse, I was
1,500 miles away from my family who had gone to "tough
it out" on a beach in Florida. My theme song as I wal-
lowed in my self-pity was "Nobody knows the trouble I've
seen. . . ."

Everything alongside the road was still in its winter
drab. I remember thinking, "What a barren place! Who
would ever want to live here?"

Then things got worse. Our bus entered a tunnel. Not
only was I cold, lonely, sick and exhausted, now I was in a
dark tunnel and could see no light at the end. Without
saying a word I slumped down in the seat and pulled my
overcoat over my head. I was miserable.

If I live to be 150 years old, I will never forget what
happened next. Without warning, we came out of the
tunnel, and it was as if we had entered another world.
Suddenly we were in the middle of downtown Pittsburgh!

There were tall buildings, people, shops, traffic lights

and even a McDonalds. I was so surprised and glad to see civilization again that I stood up and clapped. I felt like I had been delivered from a dungeon!

Freedom!

Joseph experienced something similar. He was alone, miserable and in prison. Suddenly, without any warning, he is snatched from the pit and thrust right into the middle of the action.

Genesis 41 opens with Pharaoh having two dreams he could not understand. The next day, the cupbearer tells Pharoah how Joseph had interpreted his dream accurately. Immediately Pharoah calls for Joseph to be brought before him. Joseph hears Pharoah's dream and provides an interpretation. Pharaoh's response is classic:

> So Pharoah asked them, "Can we find anyone like this man, one in whom is the spirit of God?"
>
> Then Pharoah said to Joseph, "Since God has made all this known to you, there is no one so discerning and wise as you. You shall be in charge of my palace, and all my people are to submit to your orders. Only with respect to the throne will I be greater than you." (Genesis 41:38–40)

Can you believe it? Who could have imagined that Joseph would be in the dungeon one day and be sleeping in the palace the next?

Joseph's head must have been spinning that first night. Surely he must have thought he was dreaming. Fine linens and a comfortable bed replaced his smelly prison mattress. For the first time in years, he had new, clean clothes. Pharaoh even hung a gold chain around his neck.

Instead of taking orders, suddenly Joseph had the power to command other people. In fact, everyone in Egypt except Pharaoh was subject to his decrees.

Released from prison

Monica was like Joseph. She felt trapped and could see no way out. Then the Lord set her free.

Monica's parents were teenagers who had been dating only a short time when her mother got pregnant. They were forced to get married by both sets of parents. Just a few days before Monica was born, her teenage father ran away. Monica grew up without a father, bitter because he had run out on her and her mother.

Then in her senior year of high school, she found Jesus Christ as her Savior. After graduation she felt she should attend a Christian college, and so she came to Toccoa. She became a regular attender at the Campus Church.

Although I was not sure exactly what the problem was, I could tell that Monica was troubled. I had preached several messages on Joseph and noticed her interest. She stopped me one day after class, and this is what she told me:

I was born into a home where my mom was a teen. My dad left town just before my mom gave birth. I grew up hurting and full of hate. But as I have seen how God worked in Joseph's life, I've decided to trust Him with my life too. And guess what? I decided to try and find my dad so that I could ask him to forgive me for my hatred.

After I located my father, I wrote to him, telling all about myself. And he wrote back—the first letter I ever received from him! But you know what else? He enclosed a check to pay off my tuition bill for this semester! And best of all, he is planning to meet me this next summer! Isn't that just like the Lord?

That is the way God works! He brings us out of the dungeon, saying: "I have the last word!"

Rodney discovered the same thing. He was 21 years old and had attempted suicide three times when I first met him. When I talked with him on the phone, he was in a Massachusetts hospital recovering from his latest attempt at death. But that was not his worst problem—he was also suffering from AIDS.

His voice was weak. As I talked to him about Jesus and the hope He gives, Rodney was encouraged. He admitted he was in a dungeon of despair called sin and desperately wanted out. I told him Jesus is our Deliverer, and without hesitation he prayed the prayer of repentance, claiming the cleansing of Jesus for his life. He was set free!

God provides help in even the most difficult cases

Jay Strack is another individual who discovered Jesus' power to set people free. Jay, like others we have discussed, was bitter. As a six-year-old, he saw firsthand how alcohol could destroy a home. In his book, *Shake Off the Dust*, Jay paints a vivid picture of the hurt he felt:

The warm Florida rain beat hard against the pavement as I peered out the window, waiting for my father to come home. My nose pressed against the glass, I stared ahead blankly.

"Don't worry, honey. Daddy will be here soon," Mom called from the kitchen of our suburban home.

I used to stand at the window and watch for hours, faithfully waiting for my father to come home from work. At the same time, I always wondered what he'd be like when he came in. I could remember all the times he had come home drunk, looking for a fight. When he got like that, anything could set him off. This was to be one of those days.

Time plodded on endlessly. The rain finally stopped and the muggy, humid haze of central Florida fell over the neighborhood like a thick blanket.

Finally, at dusk, a car pulled into the driveway. Dad was home! Beaming with hope, I watched Dad slowly step out of the car. But when he began to stagger up the rain-soaked driveway toward the house, my hope turned to fear.

The door burst open and the arguing began. "Where have you been all this time?" I heard Mom demand.

"None of your business," he snapped back.

Soon they were at it full blast. I ran to the doorway, clasping my hands tightly against my ears. Mom spotted me out of the corner of her eye.

"Go to your room!" she ordered. "You don't need to listen to this!" But I retreated only partway down the hall.

"I've had all I can take," Mom screamed.

"So have I!" Dad returned. "I'm leaving for good this time! There's no good reason to stay."

He can't mean it, I insisted to myself. *I must be the reason. He won't just leave us here. Surely he won't leave me too.*

But Dad began to pack his belongings and load

them into the car. Torn by disbelief, Mom watched helplessly, tears streaming down her face. She couldn't believe her husband was actually leaving for good.

"Aren't you going to change your mind?" she finally asked.

"No," he replied firmly. "This is it!" He turned and walked out the door for the final time. Unable to stand still any longer, I burst out of the house and grabbed him by the legs.

"Daddy, please don't go," I sobbed. "Please don't leave us!" He tried to be kind and held me for a moment, but finally pushed me away and drove off. My heart was broken. Tears poured down my face as I stood there feeling confused and rejected. *He will come back,* I thought. *He has to.*

"Come on in," Mom called after me. "There's nothing else we can do now."[5]

The pain continued for Jay. At age eight, he was sexually molested by a stepfather's teenage son.

Through the confusion of different men that came in and out of his home, he discovered his trust could be given to no one, not even his own mom.

Angry, tired of the struggle for identity and full of bitterness, Jay sought to be accepted by the other kids at school. Drugs were a way to get that acceptance, so they became a way of life for him. During his teenage years, he was arrested three times for possession of narcotics. Each time he was arrested, he became angrier. At this point life looked hopeless to Jay.

Growing up in Fort Myers and attending the same high school as Jay did, I remember his reputation. He was a hard-nosed wise guy who was on his way to a serious drug problem and probable time in jail.

At age 17, though, Jay was released from his pain, guilt and bitterness. He had served a three-month sentence in a detention center for wrecking a car while on LSD. Realizing he needed help, he began to search for some answers. One night he went to a small home Bible study where a youth leader spoke on how Jesus willingly died for our sin, guilt and mistakes, and how He could set people free.

Sitting there in his cutoff blue jean shorts and flip-flops, with hair to his waist, Jay began to wonder if this could really be true. He was not quite sure Jesus could forgive him for all the wrong he had done. He questioned if God would accept him, even with track marks up and down his arms from shooting drugs. What about his anger? His hate? His disappointment? "Could Jesus *really* set *me* free?" Jay thought.

What could he lose? He had tried everything else and came up empty. Jay quietly bowed his head and asked Jesus to come into his life and completely take over. Here's how he describes that moment:

> I decided to trust Someone again. I raised my hand and prayed with [the youth leader] to receive this new life. After several hours at the Bible study, I went home with a joy I'd never known. I had a peace that my past was forgiven—a new power to help with today and hope for tomorrow. I knew I would no longer be alone in my struggle. For the first time in my life I felt like I had a Father who wouldn't leave me. This time, I had a real dad! He was a spiritual Father who would meet all the needs in my life.[6]

Jay was changed completely. His senior year in high school, he led 300 teens to Christ. At age 19, he began to pastor a struggling church of 17 people in Immokalee, Florida. Within a year, 117 were saved and baptized. The attendance swelled to over 300! But that was just the beginning for this teenager once headed for trouble. He eventually came back to Fort Myers to pastor Riverside Baptist Church, and while he was there the membership climbed to over 4,000 people!

Jay is now in full-time evangelism. In 1987 more than 30,000 people responded to Christ in his worldwide crusades. He has spoken in more than 2,500 high schools and is one of the most sought-after youth speaker in America. When Jay talks about his family, drinking, drugs and how utterly senseless his life was, teens listen.

How was Jay's life changed? By the transforming power of Jesus Christ!

How about you? Do you need to be released from a dungeon? Joseph discovered that God's truth could release him from bitterness. So did Monica, Rodney and Jay. You can too.

Taking the challenge
1. What was your last "pity party" about?
2. Do you know anyone "in the pits"? How can you help them?
3. Try to think of how Joseph felt when he was released from jail. How would you have felt?
4. Is there a pit you need to be released from? Will you trust the Lord to deliver you from that dungeon?

9
Work

Quality of the Hero

Work—**something most teens** would rather not do. Some teens probably think that the word does not even exist. "Work," they say, "what's that?"

That's how Paul was. He did not attend our youth group meetings often, but when he found out we were going on a white-water rafting trip, he asked if he could go. I was glad to have him join us—at least until I saw him in action (maybe "out of action" would be a better description).

He would not help load or unload the bus, set up tents or prepare meals. The only things he managed to do were hang his hammock between two pine trees and eat. By the time we were ready to go home, everyone was fed up with his laziness. He was not asked again to go on any youth group outings.

Life requires work and lots of it. Success in school, sports and relationships depends upon how hard a person works at them. Without work, people get bored and have no goals.

My parents made sure that I was always busy. Then, I was not always thrilled about it. But now I am glad they did. I started mowing yards at age nine. I saved money for my first bike, to go to summer camps, for fishing trips and for other things I wanted that my mother would not buy me. I even worked after school every day when I was in the eighth grade to save money for a three-week trip to Japan.

The difference in Joseph's life

Joseph was a worker, and that quality made a difference in his life. Notice what Scripture says about this:

> Joseph was thirty years old when he entered the service of Pharaoh king of Egypt. And Joseph went out from Pharaoh's presence and traveled throughout Egypt. During the seven years of abundance the land produced plentifully. Joseph collected all the food produced in those seven years of abundance in Egypt and stored it in the cities. In each city he put the food grown in the fields surrounding it. Joseph stored up huge quantities of grain, like the sand of the sea; it was so much that he stopped keeping records because it was beyond measure. (Genesis 41:46–49)

Joseph had been faithful in his work habits up until the time he was appointed as Pharaoh's "vice president." Now, realizing the opportunity God had given him, he was determined to do the best job he could do. He was going to make sure he honored Pharaoh's confidence in him. And what a difference he made!

After studying Joseph's life, Jim decided to make a change in his work habits. The college cafeteria hired him as a dishwasher. He took the job seriously and made an extra effort to be thorough. His boss noticed it, and within two weeks he was promoted to another job.

Within a month, he was moved up to assistant cook and eventually to student manager of the night shift. Joseph's example encouraged Jim to do his best.

There are other passages in Scripture that tell us that we need to take our work seriously.

> Slaves, obey your earthly masters with respect and fear, and with sincerity of heart, just as you would obey Christ. Obey them not only to win their favor when their eye is on you, but like slaves of Christ, doing the will of God from your heart. Serve whole-heartedly, as if you were serving the Lord, not men, because you know that the Lord will reward everyone for whatever good he does, whether he is slave or free. (Ephesians 6:5–8)

Honoring my boss

The summer Kay and I were married, I worked on a construction crew with 120 other guys building condominiums on the beaches of southwest Florida. It was a challenge to keep my Christian witness in the presence of these men. They often took "cheap shots" at me because of my faith and joked because I desired to be faithful to my new bride.

But the toughest part was not the crew; it was the foreman, Ed. He was one of the meanest, most hard-nosed guys I have ever met. He fired people for being five minutes late to work. One day a bricklayer was standing around talking. Suddenly Ed burst out of the work trailer waving a piece of paper over his head: "Hey, you lazy, good-for-nothing! You want to stand around? Stand around and look at this! You're fired!" With that he handed the bricklayer his paycheck and headed back toward the trailer.

For the most part, we avoided Ed like he had the plague. No one wanted to come under his scrutiny. During the three months that I was there, I only saw Ed smile once—the day he announced that everybody had to stay that night and work overtime.

I dreaded talking to Ed about anything, but I was determined to honor him as my boss. I used to pray that somehow God would soften his heart so I could tell him about Christ. Before I left the job God answered that prayer.

One day I needed to leave work early. With all the courage I could muster, I went to ask Ed. He agreed but said that he would have to dock me half-a-day's pay.

When I received my paycheck the next week, it was for

the full amount. Ed had forgotten to write my time off in his ledger. I immediately went to Ed to let him know of the mistake. He was furious when I told him that I thought he had made an error, but when he looked in his ledger and saw that I was right, he melted. I will never forget what he said. "Preacher (he called me that because I was studying for the ministry) you're right. You only worked 36 hours and I paid you for 40. Thank you for your honesty. Keep the extra money."

From that day until the day I left to go back to college, Ed was my friend. If he needed supplies from town, he sent me. When there was extra money to be made, he let me know about it. On my last day, he and about 40 other men stood in line to shake my hand to say good-bye. I am convinced that their response was the direct result of my honoring Ed.

God will honor us

Joseph was committed to the people over him, and God honored him for it. And He will honor us too if we are willing to follow His standard in obeying those in authority over us.

Everyone must submit himself to the governing authorities, for there is no authority except that which God has established. The authorities that exist have been established by God. Consequently, he who rebels against the authority is rebelling against what God has instituted, and those who do so will bring judgment on themselves. For rulers hold no terror for those who do right, but for those who do wrong. Do you want to be free from fear of the one in authority?

Then do what is right and he will commend you.
(Romans 13:1–3)

How do we measure up?

Desiring to honor those in authority is one thing, but actually doing it is hard. How do you measure up? Below is a checklist that asks some important questions. See how you answer them.

1. Do I honor *everyone* in authority over me—my parents, teachers, coaches, youth leaders and others?

2. Am I on time for class and with assignments, or do I have a tendency to be late? Do I do what my parents ask me to do *when* they ask me to do it? Or do I do the things when it suits me to do them?

3. Do I meet the responsibilities given to me? Do my parents, teachers or youth leaders think of me when extra work is needed?

4. Do I look for ways of improving my performance, or am I content to carry on as usual?

5. If I was evaluated by those I am responsible to, what would they say? Improve? Doing great? Weak?

Not long ago I heard about a teen named Bill who decided to check on his job performance. He walked into a restaurant and asked if he could use the phone. The owner agreed, and Bill dialed the number of a local service station. When the voice answered on the other end, he asked: "Do you need any help at your station?" After a few moments Bill said, "I see, well okay, thanks anyway, mister."

He hung up the phone, thanked the man for letting him use it and headed for the door whistling a happy tune.

The owner called after him, "Hey, wait a minute. Didn't you just get turned down for a job? What are you so happy about?"

Bill, grinning from ear to ear, said, "Yes, I did call about a job. But the man said he already had someone. In fact, he said that the teen who worked for him now was the best he had ever had. I feel good because I'm the one he was talking about. I was just checking up on my performance!"

Joseph, Jim and Bill found out that when they obeyed God's Word about honoring those in authority over them, He honored them. I discovered it too, and so can you. Work works! And when it comes to being a hero God's way, work is a key ingredient.

Taking the challenge

1. What does the word *work* make you want to do? Pull the sheets over your head and go back to sleep?
2. Paraphrase Ephesians 6:5–8.
3. Suppose you had a boss like Ed. How would you feel? Would you want to change jobs? Pray for a change in his personality? Do you think that changes in people like Ed are possible? Do you know someone like that now? How are you handling the situation?
4. If you were to call the place where you work, what would your boss's reaction be? Would he gladly interview someone to take your place? Why or why not?
5. What were your answers to the checklist questions? What needs to be changed or improved?
6. Can you begin to develop a plan to strengthen those weaknesses? Would you be willing to sit down with your parents, teachers or other to get their input?

10

Forgiveness

Characteristic of the Hero

Have you noticed that some things are easy to do? Getting a driver's license is one example. Teens can be the poorest students in school, but when it comes to studying for and passing the driver's exam, they excel!

Being attracted to the opposite sex is another easy thing. Janet found that to be true. She had a crush on Bill in her history class, on Jeff in algebra and was wild about Allen in American literature.

Some teens find it easy to sleep until noon and beyond. Noel could do this quite easily, especially at test time. Once during midterm week, he woke up at 7:30 a.m. and remembered he had a test that day in biology. He rolled over and put his pillow on top his head. The next thing he knew, it was 4:30 in the afternoon, and his mom was fixing supper.

Other things seem next to impossible to accomplish. Keeping your parents happy is no small task. Neither is keeping your room clean. Getting through a week without rearranging your little brother's face three different ways is not easy either. Those things are hard for teenagers to do.

Forgiving those who have wronged you

There is another thing that is difficult to do. For many, it would be easier to learn to fly the space shuttle or to win the most gold medals at the next Olympic games. Why? Because doing it requires a change of heart. This difficulty is forgiving someone who has wronged you deeply.

Tom struggled with forgiving his alcoholic father. Growing up, Tom could never once remember being proud of his dad. His dad would always make a scene in a restaurant when he got drunk or say crude things to women walking down the street. Tom hated the way his father hurt his mother when he would stay out all night. He vowed to find a way to pay his dad back. Tom had his father in a "jail."

Kristi experienced the same kind of feelings. One day she came to talk to me about a problem she was having with her boyfriend. She had been dating Mike for several months. Though she felt uneasy about being with him, she missed him when they were not together.

As she shared with me, it became obvious that Kristi was not only uneasy around Mike, she felt that way about all men. Probing further, I learned that she had been sexually abused by a close relative from the time she was a child up to her early teens.

As Kristi told her story, she sobbed. She shook for nearly 15 minutes. In between the deep sobs, she cried out things like, "I hate him! I hate him so much. I wish he would come right in this room so I could spit in his face!"

For the next several weeks, Kristi met with me to talk about her past, her fears and her anger. Gradually the Lord began to change her feelings toward her relative. She could even speak his name without becoming aggressive.

Eventually she was able to see this person and say to him that all was forgiven. She released him from her "jail."

Letting the prisoners out

How do people find the courage to pardon those who have wronged them? Again, Joseph's life gives us an example to follow.

Joseph's interpretation of Pharaoh's dream came true: there were seven years of good harvest in the land, followed by seven years of famine. Because the famine affected the whole world, people from other countries came to Egypt to buy grain. Hearing that there was food in Egypt, Jacob sends 10 of his sons to buy some.

> Now Joseph was the governor of the land, the one who sold grain to all its people. So when Joseph's brothers arrived, they bowed down to him with their faces to the ground. As soon as Joseph saw his brothers, he recognized them, but he pretended to be a stranger and spoke harshly to them. "Where do you come from?" he asked.
>
> "From the land of Canaan," they replied, "to buy food."
>
> Although Joseph recognized his brothers, they did not recognize him. Then he remembered his dreams about them. . . . (Genesis 42:6–9)

Can you imagine how Joseph must have felt upon seeing his brothers again? Did he want revenge? He could have taken it, and he did throw the 10 in jail. But revenge was not his reason; he was preparing an elaborate plan to be reconciled to his family.

As events unfold, the brothers learn that this "Egyptian,"

though a strange man, is generous. He gives them the
grain they desired, plus a bonus—a sack of silver.

Finally, Joseph reveals himself to his brothers:

> Then Joseph could no longer control himself before
> all his attendants, and he cried out, "Have everyone
> leave my presence!" So there was no one with Joseph
> when he made himself known to his brothers. And
> he wept so loudly that the Egyptians heard him, and
> Pharaoh's household heard about it.
>
> Joseph said to his brothers, "I am Joseph! Is my
> father still living?" But his brothers were not able to
> answer him, because they were terrified at his pres-
> ence. (Genesis 45:1–3)

Joseph's brothers must have thought that their end was
near. Here was their brother, whom they had treated so
cruelly, the second-most powerful man in the world!

But notice what our hero says to his offenders:

> Then Joseph said to his brothers, "Come close to me."
> When they had done so, he said, "I am your brother
> Joseph, the one you sold into Egypt! And now, do not
> be distressed and do not be angry with yourselves for
> selling me here, because it was to save lives that God
> sent me ahead of you. For two years now there has
> been famine in the land, and for the next five years
> there will not be plowing and reaping. But God sent
> me ahead of you to preserve for you a remnant on
> earth and to save your lives by a great deliverance."
> (Genesis 45:4–7)

Joseph could have had them instantly killed. Yet he
forgives them. Why? Because he knows that everything

that took place was according to God's plan. Later on he tells his brothers, "You intended to harm me, but God intended it for good" (Genesis 50:20a). He is able to forgive because of God's grace in his life. He is determined to see God's plan and walk God's way, even in the toughest times!

Getting past the past, God's way

Not long ago I heard about a man named Guy who was able to forgive a deep hurt caused him by his wife. Guy grew up in Philadelphia, a member of a street gang. He learned quickly that you either win by physical force or you die.

No one messed with Guy. Once he was attacked by five members of another gang. They stabbed him a number of times, but when the fight was over, the five who attacked him were on the ground. Guy walked away bleeding, but he walked away.

Somehow despite his tough outer shell, his bitterness and his anger, God touched Guy's life. After that he changed completely. He started attending church and prayer meetings and witnessing to his old street-gang friends. Though everyone thought Guy's commitment to Jesus Christ would eventually fizzle out, he kept going strong.

Then Guy's wife left him. She had not become a Christian and wanted the old Guy back. She moved out of their house and into a mountain cabin with five of Guy's old friends.

Guy was devastated. He could not figure out why this was happening to him, especially after he had dedicated himself to the Lord. All he could think about was his wife being with the other five men and the pain that she was causing him.

But Guy rallied in his faith. The Holy Spirit ministered to him, and he was able to forgive his wife and the five friends. Eventually Guy had the chance to witness to each of them about Christ.

What a difference Jesus can make in the lives of those whose hearts have been broken by wrongs caused by others. Has someone offended you deeply? Do you ache because of abuse, someone's lies or because someone took advantage of you? Who do you need to let out of prison?

Follow Joseph's example. Not only did he forgive his brothers, he also had them move to Egypt where he could personally provide for their needs. Incredible!

Why not ask the Lord to do for you what He did for Joseph and Kristi? He loves to set people free. He will help you forget your hurts and make your life fruitful again.

Taking the challenge

1. Make a list of five things that are easy for you to do and five things that are hard. Is forgiving someone who has wronged you on the "difficult" list? What happened that makes it so hard for you to forgive the person? Do you want to get even? Why?

2. Joseph forgave his brothers. Kristi forgave her relative. What did both of them have in common that enabled them to forgive their relatives?

3. If you were one of Joseph's brothers when they discovered who he was, what would your response have been? Would you have asked for forgiveness?

4. Read Ephesians 4:32 and in your own words write out what it means. What does it say about forgiving others?

11

You

A Hero to Others

Clearly, Joseph is a hero, someone after whom we can model our lives. His life and the decisions he made reflected his dedication to being God's man. He was willing to take that risk.

What about you? Have you ever thought about being a hero God's way, an example that others could model their lives after? That decision may not be easy, but more than ever, we need real heroes who are willing to take a stand for Jesus Christ, to go against what the world says makes for a successful life.

Bud Cox came to terms with the real meaning of life. At age 23 Bud became a pro tennis player. He has played at Wimbledon, in the U.S. Open and in other major tennis events. He has had matches with McInroe and Lendl and has played doubles with Boris Becker.

With all this achievement, however, Bud has a balanced perspective of what life is really about. Recently, I talked with Bud, who attends Toccoa Falls College. His remarks were right on: "Tennis, and sports in general, are important. For many, their entire identity is in athletics. But as I see it, the Bible calls us to pour ourselves into making our lives count for Christ. That's why I left the pro circuit and came to college to train for the ministry. The only trophy that's going to be worthwhile is the trophy of seeing people come to Christ."

Saying no to the world

Going God's way means saying no to the world's ways. It means saying no to the notion that life is just one big party. The world tells us to "just relax and have fun." "Unwind, give yourself a break. You deserve it." Or we hear, "If it feels good, do it. Getting drunk? Smoking dope? Cheating? Stealing? If it's right for you, then go for it." But that lifestyle is not God's lifestyle. God is calling teens today to be heroes by His standards.

I remember hearing someone dismantle the "If it feels good, do it" lifestyle. The speaker was Bunny Martin, at one time the Yo Yo champion of the world. He started by telling about a time he had spoken at a home for unwed teenage mothers. As he talked with different girls that night, most of whom were 15 or 16 years old, he found one thing similar in their stories. Over and over again he heard the same thing: "I was told that if it felt good, do it." "My boyfriend told me that if we thought it was okay, it must be good, so we went for it. Now, like the good feeling, he's gone, and I've got the responsibility of a baby."

The more Bunny listened to those girls, the angrier he became. While driving home that night, he came up behind a car. On the car was a bumper sticker. Guess what it said? "If it feels good, do it!" Bunny went bananas.

He backed off from the car, then pushed the gas pedal to floor with all his might, crashing full speed into that car. He then backed off again and did the same thing. Crash! He smacked the car a second time. But he was not through yet. Again, he backed off, put the gas pedal to the floor and hit the car a third time.

The driver finally got control of his car and pulled off the road. Bunny pulled in behind him. The fellow jumped out of his car and started screaming at the top of his lungs, "What's the matter with you? Have you lost your mind?"

Bunny said to him, "Well, buddy, I saw your bumper sticker—'If it feels good, do it'—and after I crashed into your car the first time, it felt so good, I just had to do it some more!"

Living by this standard is ridiculous, but more than that it ruins lives. So does living by the standard of trying to please our friends.

Joni says she would be happy if she could only get the "cool" kids to like her. Tom says he would have it made if he could be on the football team. Cindi thinks she will be happy if she can only make the varsity cheerleading squad. Allen feels that the only way to really have things "together" is to hang out with the druggies in the parking lot. Joey is trying his best to impress the rich kids. Alice would be willing to do anything to be accepted by the kids in the band.

What is the result of all this? No one dares to be different!

Today's teens need real heroes

My friend Dave, a worker in Youth for Christ, shared the following facts about today's American teenagers:

In the next 30 minutes:
- 32 teens will attempt suicide
- 24 will have abortions

- 16 will become unwed mothers
- 63 will run away from home
- 207 will become alcoholics
- 21,000 will take their first drink of an alcoholic beverage
- 15,000 will use illegal drugs

God is looking for someone who will throw out a lifeline and rescue these teens. Maybe He is calling you to be that someone. Being that person takes courage; it involves taking risks, not sitting on the sidelines with your hands in your pockets.

In his book *Who Switched the Price Tags?*, Tony Campolo tells the story of Miss Thompson, a fifth-grade teacher who decided to become that kind of person.

Every year, when she met her new students, she would say, "Boys and girls, I love you all the same. I have no favorites." Of course, she wasn't being completely truthful. Teachers do have favorites and, what is worse, most teachers have students that they just don't like.

Teddy Stallard was a boy that Miss Thompson just didn't like, and for good reason. He just didn't seem interested in school. There was a dead-pan, blank expression on his face and his eyes had a glassy, unfocussed appearance. When she spoke to Teddy, he always answered in monosyllables. His clothes were musty, and his hair was unkempt. He wasn't an attractive boy and he certainly wasn't likable.

Whenever she marked Teddy's papers, Miss Thompson got a certain perverse pleasure out of putting Xs next to the wrong answers and when she put the Fs at the top of the papers, she always did it with a flair. She should have known better; she had Teddy's records and she knew more about him than she wanted to admit. The records read:

1st Grade: Teddy shows promise with his work and attitude, but poor home situation.

2nd Grade: Teddy could do better. Mother is seriously ill. He receives little help at home.

3rd Grade: Teddy is a good boy, but too serious. He is a slow learner. His mother died this year.

4th Grade: Teddy is very slow, but well-behaved. His father shows no interest.

Christmas came and the boys and girls in Miss Thompson's class brought her Christmas presents. They piled them on her desk and crowded around to watch her open them. Among the presents, there was one from Teddy Stallard. She was surprised that he had brought her a gift, but he had. Teddy's gift was wrapped in brown paper and was held together with Scotch tape. . . . When she opened Teddy's present, out fell a gaudy rhinestone bracelet, with half the stones missing, and a bottle of cheap perfume.

The other boys and girls began to giggle and smirk over Teddy's gifts, but Miss Thompson at least had enough sense to silence them by immediately putting on the bracelet and putting some of the perfume on her wrist. Holding her wrist up for the other children to smell, she said, "Doesn't it smell lovely?" And the children, taking their cue from the teacher, readily agreed with "oos" and "ahs."

At the end of the day, when school was over and the other children had left, Teddy lingered behind.

He slowly came over to her desk and said softly, "Miss Thompson . . . Miss Thompson, you smell just like my mother . . . and her bracelet looks real pretty on you too. I'm glad you liked my presents."

When Teddy left, Miss Thompson got down on her knees and asked God to forgive her.

The next day when the children came to school, they were welcomed by a new teacher. Miss Thompson had become a different person. She was no longer just a teacher; she had become an agent of God. She was now a person committed to loving her children and doing things for them that would live on after her. She helped all the children, but especially the slow ones, and especially Teddy Stallard. By the end of that school year, Teddy showed dramatic improvement. He had caught up with most of the students and was even ahead of some.

She didn't hear from Teddy for a long time. Then one day, she received a note that read:

Dear Miss Thompson:

I wanted you to be the first to know. I will be graduating second in my class.

Love,

Teddy Stallard

Four years later, another note came:

Dear Miss Thompson:

They just told me I will be graduating first in my

class. I wanted you to be the first to know. The university has not been easy, but I liked it.

Love,

Teddy Stallard

And four years later:

Dear Miss Thompson:

As of today, I am Theodore Stallard, M.D. How about that? I wanted you to be the first to know. I am getting married next month, the 27th to be exact. I want you to come and sit where my mother would sit if she were alive. You are the only family I have now; Dad died last year.

Love,

Teddy Stallard

Miss Thompson went to the wedding and sat where Teddy's mother would have sat. She deserved to sit there; she had done something for Teddy that he could never forget.[7]

Could it be that God is calling you to be the agent of change in someone's life? You do not have to be a superstar or an A student or good at sports. The only prerequisite is that you have dedicated your life 100 percent to Jesus Christ, saying, "From now on Your ways will be my ways. I'm willing to reach out to those who are hurting. By Your power, use me to set people free from their prisons. Permit me Lord, to show people the real meaning of life. I'm yours, Jesus. Do what You want with me. I want to be Your hero!"

12

Hero of Heroes!

In chapter 1 we said this study of Joseph's life would be amazing at times. The way Joseph endured all that came his way is nothing short of remarkable. No doubt, you have repeatedly said, "That's just the same sort of thing that happened to me!" It is good to know that others have gone through the same kind of things we are going through and to see that they were able to come out on top. Joseph did it through the Lord's help. Kelly found out she could too.

Kelly had been abused as a young girl by her uncle while spending the weekend at his house. She recalls how he came into her room late at night and forced himself on her. She resisted with all her might, but was not strong enough. Without saying a word to her, he repeatedly molested her, and when he was finished, he left the room. Nothing was ever said, spoken or mentioned about it again.

For years Kelly kept this to herself, too ashamed to admit what had happened. When she talked to me about it eight years later, she wept until she could cry no more.

As we talked I shared with her the things Joseph experienced, and she was encouraged. In the weeks that followed, we agreed to dig into the Bible together and find some similarities between her life and the lives of Joseph and Jesus. Though we both were familiar with these two Bible characters, we were excited about what we found.

Joseph	Jesus
Opposed evil (Gen. 37:2)	Opposed evil (Jn. 7:7)
Loved by his father (Gen. 37:3)	Loved by His Father (Matt. 3:17)
Sent by his father (Gen. 37:13)	Sent by His Father (1 Jn. 4:10)
Was conspired against (Gen. 37:18)	Was conspired against (Matt. 12:14)
Had his clothes ripped away (Gen. 37:23)	Had His clothes ripped away (Matt. 27:28)
Was put in a pit (Gen. 37:24)	Was put in a pit (Matt. 12:40)
Was sold and betrayed cheaply (Gen. 37:28)	Was sold and betrayed cheaply (Matt. 26:48)
Became a servant (Gen. 39:1)	Became a servant (Phil. 2:6–7)
Did not yield to temptation (Gen. 39:7–12)	Did not yield to temptation (Heb. 4:14–15)
Was lied about (Gen. 39:16–18)	Was lied about (Matt. 26:59–60)
Was set free (Gen. 41:14)	Was set free (Acts 2:24)
Set others free (Gen. 45:7–9)	Set others free (Jn. 8:31–32)

We came to this conclusion: Joseph is easy to identify with in many areas, but Jesus understands our pain even more. As God's Son He came to earth to bear our pain, rejection and sin and to identify with us, to become one with us. He is able to cleanse us, restore us and make us new.

Because of these things Jesus deserves to be our hero even more than Joseph does. He washes away our sin and gives us His Spirit to conquer all the hurts, emotional shreddings and times when we have been ripped off. He promises us heaven with Him for all eternity, where there will be no more hurts.

Jesus—Hero of heroes! He deserves first place in your life. Let Him be your model!

NOTES

1. Tony Campolo, *You Can Make A Difference.* (Waco, Texas: Word Books, 1984), p. 16.

2. Dr. Kevin Lehman, *The Birth Order Book.* (New York: Dell Publishing Company, 1985), p. 14.

3. Charles Swindoll, *Improving Your Serve: The Art of Unselfish Living.* (Waco, Texas: Word Books, 1981), pp. 69–70.

4. Josh McDowell, *How to Help Your Child Say "No" to Sexual Pressure.* (Waco, Texas: Word Books, 1987), pp. 33–34.

5. Jay Strack, *Shake Off the Dust.* (Nashville: Thomas Nelson Publishers, 1988), pp. 15–16.

6. Strack, pp. 28–29.

7. Tony Campolo, *Who Switched the Price Tags?* (Waco, Texas: Word Books, 1986), pp. 69–72.